Best Wishes

Joyce D. Godby

12/24/80

God Makes The Difference

Inspirational Poems by
JOYCE G. GODBY

DORRANCE & COMPANY • Ardmore, Pennsylvania

To my husband, Kimsey Ervin Godby, without whose encouragement, understanding, and patience this book would not have been written.

CONTENTS

WITH EACH SEASON
GOD SENDS HIS LOVE

YOUR TRUE AND DEAREST FRIEND

WHY ARE YOU COMPLAINING?

LET NOT YOUR HEART BE
TROUBLED—GOD CARES

POEMS THAT TELL A STORY

PREFACE

To you, the reader:

*May the contents of this book in some way bring you plea-
sure. If only one poem in this book stirs your heart to the reality
that God is and will forever be our only source of inner peace,
then I shall rejoice in my heart.*

*The poems you will read in this book were, indeed, inspired
by God, in that I have found inner peace and my eyes have
been opened to the beauty all around me, beauty that I once
took for granted, beauty that slipped by unnoticed for a long
time but, thank God, it will forever be a part of my life now.*

*May God bless you always and open your eyes to the glo-
rious wonders of the world around you. Just remember, my
friend—God Makes the Difference.*

Joyce G. Godby

God Gave Them All
to Us
for Free

NO FANCY WORDS

I cannot use the fancy words
That make a poet great,
I do not have the "know-how"
Or whatever it must take.

But the words I put on paper
Express the way I feel,
In each line my inner feelings
To the reader I reveal.

My God has truly blessed me,
And sweetly leads the way,
He is always with me
And seems to tell me what to say.

So with my pen I will try
To convey the best I can
The beauty God has shown to me
Throughout our blessed land.

No fancy words will you find
In the poetry that I write,
Just thankfulness to my Lord
For showing me the light.

Oh! I thank God for His guidance
And for His never ending love,
And for the ever flowing blessings
He sends to me from above.

When my heart is warmed by beauty
God has given me to see,
I will try to put on paper
What it has meant to me.

So if you should read a poem
That is bearing my name,
You'll know God has touched me
By His wonders once again.

GOD GAVE THEM ALL TO US FOR FREE

Life is so full of wonderful things—
Fields of daisies and birds that sing,
Flowers announcing the arrival of spring;
Yes, life is full of wonderful things.

Life is full of beauty, too,
Like a beautiful sunrise or the sky of blue,
Roses kissed by the morning dew;
Yes, life is full of beauty, too.

Life is full of things that're free—
A mountain stream, a tall pine tree,
Ears to hear and eyes to see;
God gave them all to us for free.

Life is full of happiness—
Smiles and joys and utter bliss,
A cherished memory, a warm caress;
Yes, life is full of happiness.

Life is full of hope, my friend—
Of dreams that seem to have no end,
Desires to reach love's outstretched hand;
Yes, life is full of hope, my friend.

God gave these things to us for free,
Out of love for you and love for me,
So praise God for the wonders you see;
God gave them all to us for free.

A GLIMPSE OF HEAVEN

As I looked outside this morning
At the beauty that was all around,
I caught a glimpse of heaven,
As the sun touched the dew on the ground.

The one lone rose in my garden
Sparkled with the morning dew,
It was almost as if God was telling me,
"I left this one especially for you."

It was fall and the leaves were painted
Colors of red, gold, and brown;
Who else but God could have painted like this,
I thought as the leaves floated down.

God's love filled my heart as I stood there,
With so much beauty to see;
Oh, how gracious and kind is my Savior,
And He proves it each day to me.

With a glimpse of heaven around me
I know God's plan is complete;
As I marveled at the beauty I thought,
Oh, how marvelous heaven must be.

I needed God's assurance this morning
And as usual my dear Lord came through;
A soft breeze came down and touched me,
Then I knew God had been here, too.

THEN ALL AT ONCE

Today I watched as God painted
Another masterpiece;
He painted the sky with yellow hues,
Then all at once the sun He released.

As the sun started rising, shades of pink
Seemed to mingle with the yellows there;
Across the horizon the sun spread its light,
Then all at once it was everywhere.

The sun seemed to bring the world to life;
Silhouettes vanished before my eyes;
I watched as God painted the darkened trees
Shades of green against the beautiful sky.

The untended land preceding the trees
God painted in shades of brown;
Then all at once with a few fine strokes,
Goldenrods were covering the ground.

"My cup runneth over," as my soul rejoices
At the beauty from the Master's hand;
Oh, how gracious God was just to let me watch
As His love spread across our land.

THE BLESSED OL' ROCK

Good morning, God—I knew I would find You
At our special meeting place;
So many times I've longed to be here,
Away from the hustle of life's fast pace.

As I sit on this rock overlooking the lake,
My soul rejoices once more;
For I know I'll always find You
Where the waters wash onto the shore.

O God, as I sit here and view Your world,
Forgotten are my troubles and strife;
Forgotten are the petty gripes I have
And the fast pace I travel through life.

My heart is so full of Your gracious love,
I feel nothing but peace within;
On this blessed ol' rock I find You,
Always waiting to revive me again.

From our special place I've truly been blessed;
I've watched darkness change into light,
I've watched dawn break into a beautiful day,
And watched it turn back into night.

As I look across the water at the horizon,
The sky and the waters meet;
No words can express the magnificent sight
As the sun slips into the deep.

There's a calmness surrounding this ol' rock
That I've found in no other place;
The glorious sights are etched in my mind
In a form that no one can erase.

So good morning, God, and thank You
For the solitude I always find
When I sit by the water on this rock,
That weathered the storms of time.

THE RIVERBANK

Have you ever sat on a riverbank
And fished with an old cane pole?
Oh, what peace and contentment you feel
Down deep within your soul.

It's not so much the fishing
That brings you to the riverbanks;
It's the urge you feel within your heart
To be near God and give thanks.

The beauty of nature surrounds you
And feeds your soul with God's love;
It's as if God opened a window in heaven
And out flowed His mercy from above.

The birds sing sweetly around you,
A soft breeze touches your face;
The water flows very slowly by,
As if it hates to leave this place.

It matters not that the fish are not biting,
For you're enchanted by the beauty you see;
God poured out His blessings upon you
And made your day complete.

If you have never sat on a riverbank
And fished with an old cane pole,
Then try it, my friend, and you will find
Contentment within your soul.

THE OL' TREE ON THE HILL

On a hill not very far from here
There stands a big oak tree;
With outstretched arms it stands there
For all the world to see.

God knew it would be a blessing
When He planted the seed for this tree;
Oh! How it humbles my soul to watch
As it sways to and fro in the breeze.

So stately and proud it stands there,
Overlooking the city below;
As if it were there to protect us
From harm as the years come and go.

Many times through the years God would bless me
When I climbed to the top of the hill;
Peace and contentment would fill my heart
And the presence of God I could feel.

In winter's cold God covers the ol' tree
With a blanket of purest white snow;
When you feast your eyes on this masterpiece,
Your heart is warmed by its glow.

Oh! I love this ol' tree that was blessed by God;
It shall forever be a part of me
With its outstretched arms, standing so tall,
For all the world to see.

A DAY WITHOUT GOD

Have you ever thought how it would be
To spend one day without God?
Why, I don't think I would make it;
He's my staff and He's my rod.

In times of trouble He's with me,
Whatever the hour or the day.
He's my constant companion and Savior
And He proves it in every way.

Just imagine you awoke one morning
And God was nowhere around,
No birds sweetly singing their love songs
And no flowers peeping up from the ground.

No soft breeze to blow on your face,
No trees swaying to and fro,
And the oceans and rivers were standing still
With no place for them to flow.

No God to pray to for guidance
As you faced a brand new day,
And no one to love you enough to take
All your burdens and heartaches away.

But thank God this will not happen,
For my dear Lord has proved this to me;
It may be in the smile on a baby's face
Or in the beauty God gives us to see.

As long as there's life, God will bless us
With an abundance of beauty and love.
He will pour out His blessings upon us
From the windows of heaven above.

IF I COULD

If I could I would be a great artist
And capture the wonders God allows;
I would put on canvas the beautiful sunrise
Creeping slowly from its blanket of clouds.

If I could I would capture the beauty
Of the apple tree I saw today;
I would paint the beautiful blossoms
To have when they fade away.

If I could I would paint the old farmhouse
I passed just the other day;
It was weather-worn from years gone by
But beautiful in a special way.

If I could I would put on canvas
Mountains reaching high towards the sky,
Tipped with snow, standing stately and proud
As the shimmering twilight draws nigh.

If I could, that field full of daisies
I would paint for the whole world to see,
So hearts would be warmed as mine was
By the beauty God placed before me.

If I could I would paint the great ocean,
So grand and not yet marred by man;
Where the sky seems to rest on the water
And where waves rush onto the sand.

I may never capture on canvas
The beauty of this blessed land,
But my eyes behold the works of a Master
On display every day for man.

I may never be a great artist
But I will do the best I can.
My heart has captured the beauty of God's love
And the assurance of His outstretched hand.

IF I WERE A ROSE FOR A DAY

If I were a rose for a day,
Oh, what happiness I would bring;
I would warm the heart of some dear ol' soul,
In the middle of winter I'd bring spring.

I would beautify a garden in such a way
That only a rose can do;
I would start my day as a beautiful bud,
Kissed by the morning dew.

I would thrill a young lady by my presence
In a beautiful bouquet,
Given to her by a handsome young man
In remembrance of a special day.

I would make eyes sparkle and shine with joy
As I appeared in a hospital room,
For a rose can do wonders when nothing else can
On a day filled with sickness and gloom.

If I were a rose for a day,
Oh, what joy I would spread around;
I would warm a heart, thrill a soul
And bring cheer to one that is down.

Oh, I thank God for the beautiful roses
And for the pleasure they have brought to me;
He so graciously gave the beautiful rose
For all the world to see.

THANK YOU, GOD, FOR THE TRIALS OF LIFE

Thank You, God, for the trials of life
That make me realize
Your love sustains my every need,
In You alone is where my strength lies.

Thank You, God, for lifting loads
That weigh heavily on my mind,
And for peace that comes with knowing
You are near me all the time.

Thank You, God, for stepping in
To lead when the road is rough;
When I stumble, God, You lift me up
And assist when I've had enough.

Thank You, God, for guidance
When blindly I stumble into doubt;
When I seem to have lost my way
Your hand of love reaches out.

Thank You, God, for the privilege
Of talking to You through prayer;
This blessing I cherish above others—
It matters not where I am, You are there.

Though unworthy, God, You saw fit to reveal
A glimpse of heaven in a trying hour;
You opened my eyes to the truth, O God,
And to the splendor of Your mighty power.

AS THE NEW YEAR GETS UNDER WAY

A brand new year God has granted,
It came unmarred and so pure;
Blessed by God, it appeared in the night—
Guard it well, lest you mar it for sure.

Set aside time in this new year
Just to capture the beauty at hand;
Don't take for granted God's merciful love
That he has spread throughout our land.

You need not travel far and wide
To find wondrous sights untold;
Just open your heart—God will lead you
And before your eyes the beauty will unfold.

Start with your garden on an early morn,
Where roses will be kissed by the dew;
The border of pansies with their funny faces
Will look up and smile at you.

The morning glories climbing on your fence
Will be opened by the sun's warm glow,
And the beautiful tulips of many colors
Will stand proud and erect in their row.

The grass around your beautiful garden
Sparkles like diamonds with morning dew;
Thank God for the beauty your eyes behold
And the blessings He has poured out on you.

Wherever you are God's love reaches out
To touch you in a special way;
Open your heart and receive God's blessings
As the new year gets under way.

On the Rafters of My Mind

FONDEST MEMORIES

I have stored my fondest memories
On the rafters of my mind,
Bits and pieces I have saved throughout the years;
Some go back to my childhood
When the whole world seemed so bright,
Most were happy but I've also saved some tears.

Precious moments of our early days
When it was only you and I,
Long ago before God blessed us with our boys,
Are the sweetest of my memories
And are in a special place;
I have labeled them Happiness and Joys.

Through the years the memories mounted
But I've always found the room
For the memories of our boys when they were small;
Oh, I cherish these sweet memories
And someday when I grow old,
They will be among the best ones of them all.

Our boys have grown to men now
And have made our lives complete,
And the rafters grow so heavy with the time;
As twilight shadows fall around me
I'm so thankful that I saved
My fondest memories on the rafters of my mind.

BLUEPRINT OF A HOME

Build your home with love, my child,
Without love it's only a shell;
Hold on to love all the days of your life—
It will sustain you should all else fail.

Build your foundation with faith, my child,
It will weather the storms of life;
It will crumble not when pressures mount
But stand triumph over troubles and strife.

Build the frame with hope, my child,
For hope standeth straight and tall;
It will overcome obstacles faced each day,
So let hope be your towering wall.

Build the rafters with charity, my child,
Reaching out to those with needs;
Cover the rafters with goodness and kindness
And secure them with many good deeds.

Furnish your home with prayer, my child,
Pray each day for God's help and love;
Fill each room with the many blessings
Only God can send from above.

Let your nourishment be the Bible, my child—
It will fill your soul to the brim;
Let it lead you, comfort you, and sustain your needs
Until your cup runneth over the rim.

My prayer is that God will guide you,
So that your home will stand straight and tall;
Don't alter the blueprint in any way
Lest your home will crumble and fall.

COME, MY LOVE—COME WALK WITH ME

Come, my love—come walk with me,
Hand in hand once again;
 Let's be young once more
 As in days of yore
Come walk with me down memory lane.

Let us travel back to days gone by,
Let us dwell there for a while;
 When the day breaks anew
 Let me be there with you,
And see the beauty of your smile.

Come walk with me by the beautiful lake
Where so often we have trod;
 Let us walk there once more
 On its peaceful shore
And feel the nearness of our God.

Let us travel back to long, long ago
When our arms held our first-born son;
 Nothing can compare
 To the love that was there,
For the harvest of our love had begun.

It matters not that our hair has grayed
And we move a little slower than when
 Love was in bloom
 And life played a sweet tune,
But together we can journey back then.

So come, my love—come walk with me,
Hand in hand through the golden years;
 It matters not where we go
 Just as long as I know
We'll be together as twilight nears.

CAPTURE A MEMORY

Capture a memory in the course of a day,
Remember it well, then store it away;
It should be one of happiness, never of grief,
One of joy and one that is sweet.

It's a simple thing, it has been for me,
For all around us there's beauty to see;
It may be the first flower of the season you've seen,
Peeping through the ground announcing spring.

It may be a rose, the first one to bloom;
Oh, capture this memory, a rose fades so soon;
It may be the freshness that is everywhere
After a spring rain has cleaned the air.

To capture a memory all you must do
Is remember the things that brought pleasure to you;
You don't have to travel far and wide,
For so many times it is right by your side.

It may be the smile on your baby's face
Or maybe your daughter in a gown of lace;
It may be a smile and a friendly hello
From someone you do not even know.

It may be a flower from your little son,
With a quick "I love you"—then off he will run;
Oh, a child leaves memories that will always last,
So cherish them well—a child grows up so fast.

Don't let one precious memory slip away,
Before falling asleep store them each day;
The captured memories, someday you will find,
Are your greatest possessions saved throughout your time.

TRUE VALUES

I used to want a big fine home
For entertaining guests,
I wanted it to be furnished
With nothing but the best.

I used to want a big fine yard
With gardens to impress,
So that everyone that saw them
Would marvel at the best.

My big fine home turned out to be
A bungalow filled with joys,
For God knew what I needed
And He sent us four fine boys.

My big fine yard turned out to be
The neighborhood playground,
But I never had to wonder
Where my sons could be found.

Though my home may not be tidy
Each time the doorbell rings,
It is crammed with loving memories
And joys my family brings.

My wants of long ago
Have long since vanished with the wind,
I wouldn't trade a single memory
For what I thought I wanted then.

Oh, it's strange what years can do
To change values in our mind,
With age we learn true values
That can only come with time.

OUR FIVE-YEAR-OLD BUNDLE OF JOY

We stood by his bed tonight
And watched our little boy sleep,
And felt as though our hearts would burst
With pride and humility.

O God, I prayed, please guide us
To do the things that are right,
To raise this precious angel
To be pleasing in your sight.

You trusted us, dear Lord, to raise him,
And we'll do the best we can;
If you will, please guide us—
Someday he will be a fine man.

So peaceful he lay there sleeping,
His arms wrapped around his bear;
It was hard to keep from waking him
And telling him how much we care.

Only you know how much we love him,
Our five-year-old bundle of joy,
So full of life and happiness
Is our precious little boy.

A new day will soon be dawning,
A new day to prove that we can
Take this little boy we love so much
And with your help turn him into a man.

SANTA'S GIFT

My little son taught me a lesson
I shall remember as long as I live;
The lesson he taught, I thought I knew—
It's the blessings we receive when we give.

Christmas was nearing and excitement mounting
As we wrapped gifts for this special day;
His little eyes sparkled and danced with joy
As beneath the tree each gift he would lay.

"That's the last one, son." As he took the gift,
Bewilderment I could see as he paused;
Tears came into his eyes and he said,
"Where is my gift to Santa Claus?"

"Oh Mama, Santa must have a gift,"
My precious son said to me;
"Why, he's always left me so many toys
'Neath our beautiful Christmas tree."

"And Mama, you've always told me,
It's more blessed to give than receive;
Why, Santa will think I'm a greedy boy,
If no gift for him do I leave."

I could hardly keep tears from falling
As I held my son close to me;
"The first thing tomorrow we'll go shopping,
And ol' Santa will have a gift 'neath our tree."

"We will buy special paper to wrap Santa's gift,
And it will be the prettiest one here."
A big smile came over his little face
As he wiped away a big tear.

This Christmas ol' Santa will not be forgotten,
And all the Christmases to come,
Santa's gift will be the first we purchase,
Thanks to the lesson from my precious son.

HAPPY LITTLE MEMORIES

A happy little memory
Is indeed a precious thing;
My children are all grown now
But to sweet memories I can cling.

I can have them back at any age
That I choose them to be,
From babies up to manhood
With a happy memory.

It's surprising at the memories
You have room to store,
For many years I've saved them,
Yet there is room for many more.

You can store a happy memory
Of your children as they play,
Or the way they clasp their hands
As they kneel at night to pray.

Oh, I've cherished the memories
Of each sweet and humble prayer,
One by one they named us all
And asked for God's loving care.

It's a hobby that most mothers
Tend to do most of the time;
It interferes with nothing,
For they're thoughts stored in the mind.

Oh, happy little memories
Keep loneliness away;
They're nice to have when it seems
The rain has come to stay.

Money cannot buy them
And they're worthless to a thief;
It's strange how happy memories
Wipe out the sting of grief.

Oh, a happy little memory
Is indeed a precious thing;
So start your collection
And reap the pleasures they will bring.

DEAREST MOTHER

Dearest Mother, this is your special day,
And I just had to let you know
How very dear you have been to me,
And you grow more precious as years come and go.

Your life has been sharing with others
Whatever you had at the time;
And your love has been so graciously given,
Not only to me but to all mankind.

You have never had material wealth
But, oh, Mother, how rich you are;
For your wealth has been mounting in heaven
And you are richer than most by far.

You have found the true meaning of happiness,
Which only a few ever find;
You have conquered the feeling of loneliness
By giving of yourself and your time.

You spread sunshine to those around you,
You're a living example of what God can do
When we place our lives in His hands;
His love always sees you through.

Life is truly just what we make it
And your faith will never sway;
You grow more beautiful with the years,
And I love you more with each passing day.

I want to take this opportunity
To say, "Mother, you're grand to me,"
Not just on your own special day,
But each day God allows us to see.

Your love has been a beacon to me,
Brightly shining all my life through;
As we honor mothers across our nation
I thank God for the chance to honor you.

AS I ROUND ANOTHER BEND

O Lord, please stay close by me
Through the years that lie ahead;
Help me to grow old gracefully,
With neither fear nor dread.

Instill within me patience—
This will be a trying task;
Restrain me when I'm tempted
To give advice, unless I'm asked.

Make me more aware, Lord,
That You are just a prayer away,
Should I deceive myself by thinking
I'm alone for just one day.

Give me strength to overcome, Lord,
Temptation to complain,
Should my weary mind and body
Know the agony of pain.

Help me control emotions
Should self-pity wander in;
Let those around me see, Lord,
On You alone I do depend.

If I fail at times to listen
And ramble on too long,
Whisper softly in my ear, Lord,
That I'm coming on quite strong.

Restrain me, Lord, from gossip
Should I ever stoop that low;
May I never speak an unkind word
Of either friend or foe.

When I'm tempted to find fault
Instead of good in all mankind,
Help me remember none is perfect,
And I am stepping out of line.

As my tired body weakens,
Help me accept this time of life
As a rewarding time from labor,
Not as a time that's filled with strife.

Help me, Lord, to stand alone
Without help, except from You;
If fear creeps in, I pray, Lord,
That You will see me through.

Lord, help me hold to memories
Of life when I was young,
Remembering with cheerfulness,
Not annoyed by children's fun.

Let me not forget the happiness
That I knew as a child;
If at times they are quite noisy,
Help me remember with a smile.

With Your help I'm sure I'll make it
As I round another bend;
You have never failed me, Lord,
Nor failed Your help to send.

So I ask, dear Lord, for guidance
As my senior years draw near;
Let me implant sweet memories
In the ones I love so dear.

*With Each Season
God Sends His Love*

THE VIEW FROM MY WINDOW

The view from my window changes each day,
Not a drastic change but a little in some way;
As winter disappears from the view of my window,
Spring takes over with its newness and splendor.

Once more I am blessed by the beauty of spring,
With the freshness and newness it alone can bring;
A tiny crocus has peeped through the grass
To tell me spring is here at last.

The view from my window means so much to me,
For I know all the glorious things I see
God put in view to warm my soul,
As I sit here and watch the beauty unfold.

With each season the beauty brought forth
I think is more beautiful than the season before;
In winter I marvel at the snow God sends
But I'm also thankful when spring begins.

Through the summer the view from my window brings joys,
For it's filled with happy little girls and boys;
The laughter and happiness they display
Warm my heart throughout each day.

Then fall—oh, beautiful, glorious fall!
The most colorful season of them all;
The view from my window at this time of the year
Tells me without doubt that God is here.

No words can express the way I feel
As I view the array of colors on the hill;
Red, gold, and brown and a mixture of all,
God has painted the leaves to dress up fall.

As I sit by my window I thank God above
For the splendor and beauty of His divine love;
And for eyes to see all the wonders He's placed
In view of my window, that can't be erased.

THE BEAUTIFUL SEASON OF NEWNESS

With the gloom of the world around us,
It is such a marvelous thing
That God gave us a season of newness,
The beautiful season of spring.

With the mystical, magical wonders of spring,
Love emerges from its cocoon;
And the world of gloom seems to vanish
As buds burst into bloom.

Eyes are opened to the beauty of love,
Deafened ears to the sounds that befall;
We respond to our deepest emotions,
When love beckons we answer its call.

The whole world seems much brighter
Once spring has made its debut;
It's hard to feel gloomy when eyes behold
The beauty of our world anew.

The beauty brought forth by springtime
Seems to fill my every need;
My faith is renewed in all mankind
And my heart has no room for greed.

God gave us this season of newness
And the wonders it alone can bring;
My cup runneth over with God's divine love
When it's spring—oh, beautiful spring!

SPRING IS FINALLY HERE

Spring is here—yes, it finally appeared,
Warmer weather will be along soon;
Grass is turning green, a sure sign of spring
And flowers are beginning to bloom.

My heart feels so gay now that spring's underway,
The most welcome time of the year;
Crocus peep through the grass to tell us at last
Spring is here—yes, it's finally here.

Birds are everywhere—in the trees, in the air,
Announcing the arrival of spring;
They are up before dawn, singing loud and long,
Spring is here—yes, it's here again.

Oh! The wonders I see, as conveyed to me
By God in His marvelous way,
Humble my soul as the beauty unfolds
On this warm and beautiful spring day.

God's love is so real, in my heart I feel
His presence with me today;
I thank God above for His gracious love
And for the beauty that is now on display.

EASTER DAY

Many years ago on the first Easter morn
From the grave arose Jesus, our Lord.
The huge stone that had sealed His tomb
Was rolled away—but by whom?

As three ladies visited His tomb, how they wept.
Did someone steal Jesus while the guard slept?
Then an angel told them to shed not a tear,
Saying, "Jesus has risen, He is no longer here."

The grave could not hold Him—He paid such a price
So we could someday live in paradise.
On the third day Jesus conquered the grave;
Oh, He suffered for us and His life He gave.

In Glory Land now our dear Lord awaits
To greet us all at the pearly gates;
He's prepared us a glorious place
And someday we'll see His blessed face.

Salvation is so simple—all you must do
Is believe on His name and that He died for you;
No greater love have we ever known
Than the love Jesus, our Savior, has shown.

So on this blessed Easter Day
Let each of us in our own way
Thank God for His love and for Jesus, His Son,
Who will welcome us all when this life is done.

THE SONG OF A BIRD

Oh, what a blessing God sent me today,
It came in the song of a bird;
Though I, as a human, could not understand,
My soul understood every word.

The bird was perched beside a nest
She had built high above in a tree;
And in her sweet way she was telling me,
"This is the home of my family-to-be."

From twigs entwined and bits of string
She had woven her little nest;
I could tell she was very proud of it,
And I'm sure she did her best.

God's marvelous plan amazes me so,
He left not one stone unturned;
Survival He instilled in all living things—
Who, but God, would be so concerned?

Oh, how the little bird humbled my soul
As I listened to her song today;
She was one of those many blessings
God so often sends my way.

If we sang praises as the little birds do,
What a joyous sound it would be;
For all that we are and all that we have
God supplied for you and for me.

THANK GOD, THANK GOD—HE LOVES YOU

I was awakened this morning by the song of a bird
Outside my window, perched high in a tree;
How happy he sounded as he sang—
Wake up, wake up—come and see.

As I opened the door and looked outside
I knew why he sang so loud;
The sun was creeping from beneath
A beautiful fluffy pink cloud.

I watched the bird as it fluttered around,
Still singing as loud as could be;
Oh, how great is God's love and goodness
And how sweetly He conveys it to me.

The sun had climbed high and the cloud was gone,
What a beautiful day this would be!
God gave so much to fill my life—
Oh, how gracious God is to me.

He sent the little bird to wake me,
He sent the beautiful sunrise, too;
As I looked up the bird flew by singing,
Thank God, thank God—He loves you.

THE DAISY THAT STOOD ALL ALONE

In a field full of daisies one stood alone
Trying hard just to stay alive;
Tall grass surrounded it, almost hiding it,
Yet the daisy fought hard to survive.

Off in the distance many grew in abundance,
Towering high above the tall grass;
Grouped together and thriving quite well,
There was no doubt in my mind they would last.

But the one lone daisy I had doubts about
Was much smaller than all the rest,
Yet to me it was the most beautiful,
Because I knew it was giving its best.

As I stood there admiring the little daisy,
I felt a warmth in my heart and I knew
God had proven to me you can stand alone
Enduring hardships we're often put through.

The daisies in bunches were beautiful without doubt,
Because they too were made by God's hand,
But the little daisy proved with God's help
One alone can take a firm stand.

It's much easier when we all pull together,
But in God's eyes there's none too small
To weather the storms that go with life,
And with His help we can all stand tall.

I pulled the grass away from the daisy
And packed the soil so it would not fall;
It had been such an inspiration to me,
Now the little daisy can be seen by all.

THE BEAUTIFUL LITTLE BUTTERFLY

A beautiful butterfly landed
On the ground beside my chair;
It sat there for a minute,
Then gracefully took to the air.

As it fluttered around with grace and ease,
It was as though I were watching a play;
It seemed this little butterfly
Was dancing a planned ballet.

When it had finished its performance
It seemed to bow, then it took to flight;
All through the day its beauty remained,
For it brought unto me sheer delight.

Oh, beautiful little butterfly,
So elegant, with velvet wings,
You must have been very special to God,
For your apparel is fit for kings.

God dressed you up like royalty,
And dignity you possess;
You glide through the air so gracefully,
As if in utter bliss.

You draw attention wherever you go,
From the young as well as the old,
When you light and display your colors
Of orange, yellow, brown, and gold.

Oh, beautiful little butterfly,
Do you know what you are today?
You are one of the special blessings
God's always sending my way.

WINTER

O Winter, with your blanket of fluffy white snow,
From your chilling breath the cold winds blow,
But I marvel at the beauty you spread all around.
O Winter, you've made a wonderland of our town.

I have watched you come for many years,
To most you bring joy but to some you bring tears;
O Winter, you have made eyes sparkle and shine
With your unsurpassed beauty, time after time.

Children are thrilled when they awake
To snow-covered hills and iced-over lake;
Skiers speed down the snow-covered slope,
And ice skaters glide on the lake below.

O Winter, in your splendor and beauty untold,
Many suffer immensely from your bitter cold;
Many dread your appearance from year to year,
To them you mean hunger, suffering, and fear.

O Winter, with your beautiful blanket of snow,
With your chilling breath, you soon must go;
You will be replaced by the flowers of spring,
But welcomed back as the Christmas bells ring.

THE FIRST SNOWFALL OF THE SEASON

I awoke this morning to a calmness
That only a snowfall can bring;
It seemed the world was in reverence
To honor the snow once again.

As I lay listening, not a sound could I hear,
So I went to the window to see;
Oh! The beauty I saw as I stood there
Filled my soul with humility.

In the still of night God covered our town
With a blanket of fluffy white snow;
And the trees—oh, how pretty they were,
Laden with snow and bowing down low.

The first snowfall of the season
Always fills my heart full of joys;
As yet its beauty had not been touched
By happy little girls and boys.

But it won't be long before they awake
And see the beauty of this wonderland;
For a while they will marvel in amazement
Then all at once they'll announce their plan.

They will dance with joy as they bundle up,
Their eyes will sparkle and shine;
Out from hiding will come shiny sleds
That haven't been seen for a long, long time.

Soon the snow will have tracks made by sleds,
And imprints of children's feet;
The calmness of this dawn will soon disappear
With laughter of children as they meet.

The serenity I feel as I look around
Is a gift God sent my way;
He awoke me early to see the sight
Before the children start their day.

ONE SNOWY MORN

Snow lies still upon the ground
In a quiet and peaceful way;
Icicles hang from eaves of the roof
And the sky is shades of gray.

The creek that runs behind the house
Is stilled by the snow and ice;
The serenity of this beautiful morn
Would be an artist's paradise.

Tree branches cradle the new-fallen snow
As a mother would cuddle her child;
No footprints yet mar this carpet of white
That stretches for many a mile.

With the purity of the snow
Come peace and tranquility;
For me it's a symbol of God's divine love
And a covenant between God and me.

I'm so thankful for the privilege of seeing,
For words, I now realize,
Could not describe the beauty
That now lies before my eyes.

With the calmness all around me,
God's love fills my heart to the brim;
The sight my eyes are beholding
Could have come from no one but Him.

Your True and
Dearest Friend

YOUR TRUE AND DEAREST FRIEND

How well do you know Jesus,
Your true and dearest friend?
Would you recognize your Savior
Well enough to let Him in?

Would your heart beat fast with joy
If you opened your door wide
And Jesus stood there smiling?
Would you welcome Him inside?

Would you hesitate and wonder—
Have I met this man before?
Would He have to introduce Himself
Before you let Him through the door?

Could you talk to Jesus face to face
In just the way you pray?
Or would you stumble trying to find
The right words for you to say?

If these words start you to wonder,
Then you should search your heart today,
For Jesus is surely coming
And the time's not far away.

Don't put off until tomorrow
The salvation of your soul,
For we know not the hour
Or the time the bells will toll.

So if Jesus knocks upon your door,
With outstretched arms bid Him come in,
For He loved you more than life itself;
He is your true and dearest friend.

HE STOOPED LOW ENOUGH
TO SAVE SOMEONE LIKE ME

I felt the burdens of the world upon my shoulders,
I felt a great desire to be alone;
It was hard for me to smile at those around me,
It was hard for me to manage on my own.

Then one day I knelt and prayed, "O blessed Jesus,
Will you stoop low enough to save someone like me?"
Then in the distance I could hear my Savior saying,
"You're forgiven—now rise and follow Me."

Then Jesus came and lifted all my burdens,
He removed my doubts and washed away all sin;
Upon his blessed shoulders lay my burdens,
Then so graciously He gave me peace within.

It was hard to comprehend God's mighty power,
For sin had blinded me till I could hardly see,
But as I knelt, I felt His Holy Spirit
Fill the room and stand there over me.

Now at last my eyes are opened to God's power,
And my soul at last is free of doubt;
Oh, thank God, through faith He has redeemed me,
And that's what salvation is all about.

Now and then I stumble but I'm trying,
And I have the love of God within;
I wonder now just how I ever made it
Before Jesus saved me from a life of sin.

TAKE NOTHING FOR GRANTED

It's sad how we all take for granted
Good health, day after day,
Until we awake one morning and find
Our good health has been taken away.

Not until then do we realize
How precious God's gift had been;
Then frantically we begin to pray,
Asking God to restore it again.

So much in life we accept without thanks,
Yet God's blessings flow on and on;
I'm sure at times our Lord must think
Our hearts are turning to stone.

We don't hesitate to call on Him
When we're faced with problems in life;
He is always the first one we call on
To relieve our heartaches and strife.

Just how much do you take for granted?
Do you thank God for the air you breathe?
Do you thank Him for your good health?
For out of love He supplies each need.

The clothes we wear, the roof over our heads,
And even the food we eat,
God supplies a way for those that try
And for those there is no defeat.

So thank God for His merciful love
And for supplying your needs each day;
Take nothing for granted, life just does not happen—
Our blessed Lord planned life this way.

THE RICHEST MEN IN THIS WORLD

The richest men in this world
Do not drive fine limousines,
Nor do they live in mansions
Or wear large diamond rings.

They are not much on entertaining
Nor do they drink fine champagne;
They do not feast on caviar
And over servants reign.

They do not envy their fellow man
The "finer things of life,"
For the richest men in this world
Toil daily with troubles and strife.

They have no need for modern banks
To handle their riches or fame;
For the broker that handles their affairs
You will find is one and the same.

They store their riches in heaven,
Where thieves cannot break in;
It's guarded each minute of every day
By Jesus, our Savior and King.

So the richest men in this world
To most are not well known;
But they are heirs to God's kingdom,
With mansions around God's great throne.

NO DOUBT IN MY MIND

How could anyone doubt God's power
When they marvel at the mountains high,
Or stand on a beach and gaze at the ocean,
As the sun sinks low in the sky?

How could anyone doubt God's greatness
When they gaze at a beautiful tree?
So graceful and proud it always stands
For anyone that is willing to see.

How could anyone doubt God's presence
With all the beauty He spreads around?
I feel His presence when a soft breeze blows
Or when a crocus peeks through the ground.

How could anyone doubt God's blessings
That fall like rain on our lives each day?
Blessings we so often take for granted,
And most time no thanks do we say.

How could anyone doubt God's endless love
When they look upon their baby's face?
Oh, the warmth that is felt within the heart
Is just a touch of God's love and grace.

How could anyone doubt God's mercy,
When He sent Jesus, His own blessed Son,
To pave the way to our eternal home?
No greater love to us will come.

Oh, there's no doubt in my mind God loves me,
In some way He reveals it each day;
I feel His presence, His love, His power, and His greatness
By the blessings He sends my way.

LIVE ONLY FOR TODAY

Dread not tomorrow, live only for today,
For in a fleeting moment it will pass away;
Plant seeds of love that will grow and bear
Fruits of kindness that will spread everywhere.

We're not promised tomorrow so leave memories behind,
To be cherished forever while there is time;
Seeds of love will flourish, there's no doubt,
And love is what living is all about.

Spread sunshine and kindness to those in despair,
Let them know today that you really care;
For another dawn may never break,
So plant your seeds of love before it's too late.

Give someone a smile in the course of the day,
It costs you nothing but goes a long way.
A kind word spoken to some lonely soul
Could mean more to him than silver or gold.

Sharing with others the blessings received
Will insure happiness that comes with each deed;
So dread not tomorrow, live only for today,
Always doing your best every step of the way.

OH YE OF LITTLE FAITH

"Oh ye of little faith"—
How often these words ring
Within my heart, within my soul,
When dealt life's bitter sting.

Yet deep inside within my heart
I know my God is there;
Whenever I need Him most
He hears my every prayer.

When sorrows come and burdens mount
And the road of life is rough,
He never fails to intercede
When He knows I've had enough.

The human weakness of a man,
When tested, you will find,
Cries out for strength and guidance
To ease his troubled mind.

Tired and weary from the pace of life
That we must travel day by day,
Like a clinging vine the pressures
Hold tightly, come what may.

When I've struggled through a day
And taken all that I can take,
I seem to hear a sweet voice whisper,
"Oh, ye of little faith."

If my vision's blurred with tears
Until I can no longer see,
God wipes the tears from my eyes
With His sweet words "Come unto Me."

TRY GOD TODAY

If you feel the load you now bear
Is much too heavy but no one's aware,
If the burdens you carry are dragging you down,
You've searched for help but none can be found—
    Try God today.

When depression is fast closing in on you,
If you've cried for relief and know not what to do,
When you have lost faith in all mankind,
You should make amends; there is still time—
    Try God today.

If your body is tired and gripped with pain,
With no relief in sight and you've tried everything,
If there is no end to your daily task
And you don't know how much longer you'll last—
    Try God today.

Now's the time to get on your knees and pray,
Submitting yourself to God's will today;
Believe in your heart He will work it out,
But be sure you leave no room for doubt—
    Try God today.

God's endless love will reach out to you,
Let Him rule your life and you'll find this true:
Depression will vanish and you'll find peace within
Once God has cleansed you of all sin—
    Try God today.

You will soon find good in mankind once more
And your daily task will not be such a chore;
He'll lift the load because He cares for you,
There is nothing impossible for God to do—
    Try God today.

Just believe on His name; He'll set you free
Of trials and troubles that won't let you be;
So try God today, you have nothing to lose
But so much to gain if God's way you choose;
Try God today.

THANK YOU, GOD, FOR ALL YOU DO

Thank You, God, for the air we breathe,
And for the flowers and for the trees;
Thank You for the warm gentle rain
And the sun that brings them to life each spring.

Thank You, God, for Your tender care,
And for Your presence everywhere;
Be it night or day You are always here,
Thank You, God, for being near.

Thank You, God, for the brooks and streams
And the beautiful birds and the songs they sing;
They fill our hearts full of gladness each day,
Thank You, God, for Your gracious way.

Thank You, God, for the tranquility I feel
As I watch the sun rise over the hill;
As it slowly rises I know in my heart
Just how great, oh God, You are.

Forgive me, dear God, if I fail one day
To thank You for all that You send my way;
There's so much we all take for granted, I know,
Yet You keep on giving and loving us so.

Thank You, God, for all that You do
To show us Your love is real and true;
As I gaze at the beauty on every hand,
I know without doubt You have blessed our land.

AT LAST I SEE

"Ask, and it shall be given you;
Seek, and ye shall find;
Knock, and it shall be opened unto you"—
Today this message came to my mind.

It was one of those days when I felt alone,
Yet I was surrounded by family and friends;
So this message my Savior sent to me,
The message He so often sends.

"Ask," my Savior was telling me,
And this I had not done;
I was trying to go through my busy day
Without help from anyone.

"Seek," my Lord was saying,
Yet I had gone through most of the day
Accepting life the way it was
Without seeking help along the way.

"Knock," my Master had said to me,
"And it shall be opened unto you,"
Yet, none of the things had I done,
Not a single one He had told me to do.

I started my day without asking
For guidance from my blessed King,
I just rushed into my busy day
And could not accomplish a thing.

I did not seek as I was told,
Therefore, I did not find
The strength I needed so badly,
And I got further and further behind.

I did not knock as I was told,
So it was not opened unto me;
Oh! How foolish I had been this day,
But, thank God, at last I see.

I fell upon my knees and prayed,
"Oh, Lord, at last I see;
I am asking for help and seeking guidance,
Please open Your door to me."

Now with the dawning of each new day,
I pray for guidance from above,
For I will not face another day
Without God's help and much-needed love.

I KNELT AT THE CROSS OF CALVARY

"Come unto Me," Jesus said to me,
So I knelt at the cross of Calvary;
"Oh, Jesus, I'm not worthy to look on Your face,"
But there on my knees I received his grace.

"I'm a sinner, O Jesus, and not worthy of
Your mercy and most of all Your love."
I poured out my heart and soul that day,
Then Jesus washed all my sins away.

"None is perfect, no, not one,"
Was the reply I received from God's only Son;
"Follow me." Then I felt peace within,
As my soul was released from the bondage of sin.

If Jesus will save a sinner like me,
Through faith He'll save you if you trust and believe;
Repent of your sins and believe on His name;
God sent us his Son and He bore our shame.

Yes, He bore our sins when He shed His life's blood,
You can search but you'll find there's no greater love;
And no greater gift will you ever receive
Than the gift of salvation when you repent and believe.

Oh, the message our blessed Savior brought
Was the message my weary soul hath sought:
Believe on My name and repent of all sin,
And walk no more in darkness again.

Thank You, dear Jesus, for saving such as me,
From a life of torment You've set me free;
I know without doubt I am heaven-bound,
My soul was lost but, thank God, it's been found.

ON THE WINGS OF GOD'S LOVE

On the wings of love God has ushered in
Another brand-new day;
So fresh its fragrance, so peaceful its sound
And so perfect in every way.

The dawn of this day, the first break of light,
Is filled with serenity thereof;
This time of the day awakens souls
To the awareness of God's divine love.

This day will be blessed by the sun's warm rays;
It is now rising into view,
And its rays beam down upon the earth
Lightly touching the morning dew.

God leaves with us this beautiful day
With no promise that another He'll send;
What we do with this day is up to us—
It is ours from the start to the end.

Don't waste the new day God has sent us
With all the splendor and beauty from on high;
On the wings of love God will take it away
As the twilight shadows draw nigh.

Why Are You Complaining?

WHY ARE YOU COMPLAINING?

You say the faucet's dripping
And the laundry is piled high;
It seems that all your baby does
Is eat and wet and cry.

You say that company's coming
And you forgot to thaw the steak;
The phone has rung all morning
And how much more can you take?—

Just sit down for a minute—
There is something I must say,
And when I've finished talking
You can finish out your day.

Now a dripping faucet's pesty,
But stop and think, my friend;
What if you had no water?
You would have a problem then.

And now your precious baby—
He sounds normal as can be,
All he needs is your assurance,
Give him love and you will see.

You say that company's coming
And you forgot to thaw the meat;
Again, my friend, be thankful
For your friends and food to eat.

So your phone has rung all morning
And your nerves are all ajar,
But at least you are not lonely
As so many people are.

Think of what I've said to you,
Then fall down on your knees
And thank God for His goodness—
He's supplied you with your needs.

Now you can cook the steak while frozen;
It will turn out just as good;
But tomorrow start your day off
With God's help, the way you should.

TRY JUST A LITTLE HARDER

Try just a little harder
To be a better you;
Strive to brighten up the day
Of someone that's sad and blue.

Let the love of God speak through you
With every word you speak today;
Try just a little harder
To help someone find his way.

Try just a little harder
To let others know you care;
If the load they bear is heavy,
Offer help, their load to share.

Let the love of God shine in you,
Brighten up some lonely soul;
For at times a kind word spoken
Can indeed mean more than gold.

Try just a little harder
To be a better friend each day;
Don't wait in the shadows,
They may need your help today.

We never really understand
The needs of those around,
Unless we make it known to them
We're willing to be found.

So extend a helping hand today
To those who do have needs;
Share what you have with others,
And strive each day to do good deeds.

Try just a little harder
To be a better you,
Always do the best you can,
As God would have you do.

WHAT DID YOU DO FOR GOD TODAY?

Just take a moment from your busy day
And think what did you do for God today?
Did you thank Him for keeping you safe through the night,
When you awoke to the morning light?

Your precious baby you hold close to you
Was a gift of love—God gave him, too;
As you look into his innocent face,
Do you thank God for His bountiful grace?

Did you thank God when you looked outside
At the wonders that surround you on every side?
That rose in your garden with a fragrance so sweet,
God tends and cares for at night while you sleep.

Did you thank God for His gracious love,
And for Jesus, His Son, whom He sent from above
To save us from sin and show us the way
To that beautiful city in a land far away?

Without God's love, where would you be
When this life is over and you face eternity?
When you stand before God on the great judgment day
And He calls your name, what will you say?

What did you do for God, dear friend?
He gave you life, He cleansed you of sin.
Oh, love Him and thank Him for His merciful grace,
Then someday you can thank Him, face to face.

ONE RAINY DAY

As I awoke this morning
I thought, "What a gloomy day;
I cannot do the things I planned,
This rain stands in my way."

I was feeling sorry for myself
When a voice from deep within
Seemed to whisper soft and tenderly,
"Another day, the sun I'll send.

I sent this rain to a farmer
Who needed it very bad;
If his crop did not get rain
He would lose everything he had.

Then a little old lady so humble
Asked, if I did not mind,
To send enough rain to fill her well
Whenever I had the time.

A forest fire was raging
Just outside your town,
My people were fighting very hard
But could not slow it down.

So I sprinkled it from heaven,
Now My children won't be hurt;
They kneel to give Me heartfelt thanks
In the charred and blackened dirt.

I'm sorry if I offended you,"
The soft voice seemed to say,
"But tomorrow I will send the sun
To brighten up your day."

I fell on my knees and prayed,
"O God, will You forgive
The selfishness I've shown this day;
You've just taught me how to live.

Oh, I promise You, dear Lord,
Whatever You send my way
I will accept with a thankful heart,
And remember this rainy day."

A PRICELESS GIFT

If you are blessed with a real true friend,
You are one of the fortunate few;
Guard this friendship with all that you have
And don't trade it for one that is new.

It's a priceless gift with no strings attached,
And grows more priceless as the years come and go;
Don't confuse the worth of this precious gift
With a friendship that is only for show.

The worth of a friend can't be measured,
It's worth more than a mountain of gold;
It's worth more than a mine full of silver,
And can never be bought or sold.

A friend is worth more than diamonds
No matter how they sparkle and shine;
He's worth more than a sea full of pearls
And almost as hard to find.

In order to have a real true friend
You must be one in return;
A one-way friendship is no friendship at all,
And this lesson is one you will learn.

Thank God if you are blessed with a real true friend,
And cherish his worth every day;
For friendship is one thing we must earn—
Guard it well lest it slip away.

TOMORROW WILL BE DIFFERENT

I made it through the day, Lord,
But it was hard to do,
I started it off hurriedly
Without a talk with You.

The hassle was unreal, Lord,
Throughout the entire day,
But the thing that hurts me most now,
I wished Your day away.

I let frustrations rule my day
But this was my fault too,
I didn't take the time, Lord,
To be assured by You.

I simply did not listen,
So indeed I did not hear;
The songs the birds were singing
Fell on my deafened ear.

I did not look around me,
So indeed I did not see
The wonders of Your love
That You put here for me.

I was too busy with my problems,
Trying to solve them all alone,
So I did not see my blessings
Until the day was almost gone.

I didn't take the time for beauty
And I did not stop to pray,
My problems were my making
And I wasted this sweet day.

I did not ask for guidance,
So, Lord, You let me be;
I did not ask for patience,
So You sent none to me.

I did not thank You, Jesus,
For the safety of Your love,
When I awoke this morning,
I cast not my eyes above.

I did not accept Your blessings—
They fell on my hardened heart;
So You let me try it on my own
Right from the very start.

O Lord, will You forgive me
For the impatience I have shown?
Without Your help I fell apart
And could not make it on my own.

Oh, tomorrow will be different,
And thank You, Lord, for Your sweet care;
I will meet You here tomorrow—
I will meet You here in prayer.

Let Not Your Heart Be Troubled—God Cares

GOD IS THE ANSWER

*In each life there will be times
When sorrow weighs heavily on our minds;
In this life many burdens we must bear,
But of each burden God is aware.*

*God will mend your broken heart
And ease the pain that tore you apart;
God will give you strength from above
To carry on because of His love.*

*God will ease the hurt and dry your tears
And leave sweet memories throughout your years;
He will lift you up when you are down,
He is your true friend when none can be found.*

*Life on this earth is but a stepping stone
To that beautiful city, our eternal home.
There will be no parting and no more pain
In heaven where God will forever reign.*

*So grieve not, dear friend, your loved one awaits
In that beautiful city with the pearly gates,
Where streets are paved with purest gold
And throughout eternity we will never grow old.*

*God will not forsake you—death is His plan
By which we must journey to the promised land.
Through God's merciful love and by His grace
Someday we will meet Him face to face.*

LET ME LEAN ON YOU, GOD

Let me lean on You, God,
The road is steep and rough;
I can no longer find my way
And God, I've had enough.

Day after day I've stumbled
On this rugged road I've trod;
There's no end and I'm so weary—
Oh, will You help me, God?

My confidence is gone now,
The night of life has settled in;
And the rugged road I travel
Seems now to have no end.

If you'll lead me, God, I'll follow
Down the endless road of strife;
Let me once more see the beauty
Of the brighter side of life.

So please let me lean on You, God,
Won't you lead me safely home?
Within my heart I know now
I can't make it on my own.

MY BLESSED LORD CARES

God cares if our hearts are saddened
By events that come our way,
He cares if the burdens we carry
Are much too heavy today.

God cares if the pace of this life
Is more than we can stand,
He cares and if we only ask
He will lend us a helping hand.

God cares if we are weary
From a life of sorrow and pain,
He cares and that is the reason
His blessings fall on us like rain.

God cares—that is why He sent Jesus,
His only begotten Son;
To relieve the pain and suffering,
And tell us of things to come.

Jesus died because He loved us;
He suffered to save such as me;
He shed His life's blood for my sins
When they nailed Him to Calvary's tree.

He's prepared us a place called heaven,
And in heaven no pain will we bear;
By God's merciful grace we will enter
Because He cares—and will always care.

JESUS SWEETLY HOLDS ONTO HIS HAND

He has traveled through the valley of death
With no fear as his journey ends;
For Jesus sweetly holds onto his hand
As his entry into eternity begins.

Although your heart is saddened with grief,
In the days to come you will find
God will help you bear your heavy load
And bring peace to your saddened mind.

Jesus promised He'd prepare for each of us
A place when this life is o'er;
A beautiful mansion awaits us,
But we must first reach that far-off shore.

In that glorious city called heaven
Heartaches and sorrows cannot enter in;
Only joy and happiness await us there,
With no parting ever again.

When sorrows weigh heavily on our hearts,
And there is so much we don't understand—
The why and the reasons of it all—
Try to remember it is part of God's plan.

The empty space left cannot be filled
But thank God for the assurance He sends,
We'll be reunited with our loved ones
Someday when our life's journey ends.

HE BECKONED

God reached out His hand of love to her,
He beckoned and she answered His call;
Together they walked through the valley of death
Where the darkest of shadows befall.

Her spirit emerged triumphantly,
For our Savior held onto her hand;
He led her and she followed Him
Until they reached the promised land.

She has crossed the raging waters of life,
She has reached that far-off shore;
Now she will rest in the arms of our Savior,
Where suffering will be no more.

Though your heart is saddened by your loss,
God's love will abide with you,
For He gives us the blessed assurance
That where we are, He will be there too.

The empty space left cannot be filled,
But in the days to come you will find
That God alone can erase your grief
And bring peace to your saddened mind.

The tears in your eyes will vanish,
God will comfort and ease the pain;
Sweet memories will replace your sorrow
And in your heart they will remain.

The why and the reason we don't understand,
But God assured us this is not the end;
It is only the beginning of eternity,
Where there will be no parting again.

GARDEN OF LIFE

In the garden of life God plants tiny seeds,
Then from heaven He watches as they thrive;
From God's garden come the finest of roses
That bring beauty and love to our lives.

From the garden of life God picks the roses
To adorn His beautiful throne;
Every now and then the rose He picks
Is a bud, not yet fully grown.

Today God picked a rose from His garden
To place in His heavenly bouquet;
The rose He picked was only a bud,
But was perfect for His beautiful array.

The bud God picked He had nourished
And tended with loving care;
The soil was the finest where it grew
And its beauty was very rare.

Though the beautiful bud was cherished on earth
And will never burst into full bloom;
God recognized the splendor of the little bud,
That's why He picked it so soon.

The rose will be missed from the garden,
But God's roses never die;
For we too someday will be picked by God
And shall adorn His bouquet in the sky.

Poems That Tell a Story

AN OLD MAN'S HUMBLE PRAYER

Down the road not far from me
An old man lived alone;
He was as good a person
As I have ever known.

I visited with him often,
He was such a joy to me;
Although his face was wrinkled,
An inner beauty you could see.

I never knew the loneliness
The old man felt until today,
As I stood at his open door
And heard the old man pray.

The prayer the old man uttered
I remember until this day,
So humbly he talked to God,
And this is what I heard him say.

"Yesterday, Lord, You sent the rain,
The slow and gentle kind,
And today You sent the sun—
Now everything's looking fine.

The grass is so much greener
And so are the leaves on the trees,
Everything looks so much brighter now;
O, Lord, You're so good to me!

Remember my little garden, Lord,
Since the rain it's coming 'round;
Why, I could hardly believe my eyes today—
The beans are peeping through the ground.

It wasn't very long ago
That I planted the tiny seeds,
But of course You remember, Lord,
You had to help me off my knees.

Why, I thought I wasn't gonna make it,
That was before I called on You;
It seemed just like You lifted me up—
Without Your help, Lord, what would I do?

You know, Lord, I was just thinking
What a joy it would really be
If You came for a visit
And stayed a while with me.

Why, there's so much we could talk about,
We've been friends a long, long time;
We might stay up half the night
Just talking, if You didn't mind.

I guess You think I'm greedy, Lord,
But I don't mean to be;
It's just I get so lonesome now
Since there's no one here but me.

The kids have all left home now,
And, Lord, they turned out fine;
I recall when they were small
You helped me out time after time.

And Mama! Lord, I miss her
Since You called her home to rest;
Now please don't get me wrong, Lord,
You've always known what's best.

I know someday I'll join her
When my task is finished here,
And that's what keeps me going—
That and knowing You are near.

Well, Lord, I better let You go,
You're such a busy man;
But thank You, Lord, for listening
And for Your blessings, Lord. Amen."

God must have heard every word
The old man had to say,
For his task on earth is finished—
God took him home that day.

Loneliness will be no more
For that dear ol' soul;
God knew he was a righteous man
With a heart as pure as gold.

The old man wouldn't come right out
And ask God to take him home,
But God looked inside his heart and knew
The old man felt so alone.

Now I'm sure the old man's happy
Since God reached out His hand of love,
And took him home to be with Him
In His mansion up above.

GOD WILL WEAR THE ONLY CROWN

Don't let the stars you now wear in your crown
Throw you off balance and bring you to the ground;
Watch for a storm that could come anytime
And sweep you off that beautiful cloud nine.

With your head held so high it is hard to greet
The ones you step on beneath your feet;
And the ones you now walk on made you what you are,
They paid a price for each precious star.

As your stars glitter, sparkle, and shine,
It would be well for you to keep in mind
That in God's eyes there's none large or small,
He's not partial to one—He loves us all.

Stop and think as you try to balance your crown:
In the process of climbing did you push someone down?
God intended for us all to do our best,
But it's wrong to hurt others while feathering our nest.

It takes all kinds of men to make this world turn,
And it takes a lot of listening in order to learn;
Do unto others as you would have them to do—
This is well to remember all your life through.

Remember, too, as you tread life's road,
It's well and good to set a high goal,
But tread slowly lest you step on one of God's own,
For the final judgement will be God's alone.

I too wore the star-studded crown of success
And respect for others I did not possess;
One morning I awoke on the brink of despair
And prayed "O God! Please hear my prayer.

Please remove this crown that has caused so much grief,
And deliver me from this life of deceit."
I begged for forgiveness for the errors of my way
And God graciously answered my prayer that day.

He removed the crown and washed away all sin,
He cleansed my soul and made me whole again.
Now each day of my life I shall tell of God's grace;
He removed the barriers I would surely face.

So don't let the stars you now wear in your crown
Cause you total destruction and drag you down;
Please heed my advice before it's too late—
Take stock of your life and correct each mistake.

When this life is over and we face judgement day,
God will wear the only crown and will have the last say;
So prepare for this day: take care that you store
Riches in heaven—they will be worth so much more.

THE VOICE

"Yes, Lord," I heard myself saying,
"Was it You that called my name?"
I listened closely but all I could hear
Was rain splattering against my window pane.

Now why, I thought, did I say such a thing?
Yet it seemed as natural as could be
To answer the voice I thought I heard
As that of my Savior calling me.

I went to the door—no one was there,
Not one single soul in sight;
I looked all around but all I could see
Was a beautiful bird in flight.

All day long I pondered on this—
The voice I thought I heard;
There was really no logical answer,
So to my family I uttered not a word.

Several weeks passed when I was awakened
Out of a sound sleep just before dawn;
I went outside and walked through the garden
While the dew lay still on the lawn.

The sun slowly rose from its resting place,
Sending rays to each dewdrop in sight;
Oh, they sparkled and glistened at the rays' warm touch,
And the flowers lifted their heads to the light.

A soft breeze was blowing against my face,
There was a sweet smell of spring in the air;
Oh! How beautiful, I thought, is this time of the year;
God's love can be seen everywhere.

Upon turning around once more I heard
A voice softly speaking my name,
And again I answered as I had before
For the voice was one and the same.

Just as before, I looked all around
And again not a soul could I see;
Then from out of nowhere came the beautiful bird,
This time it flew closer to me.

Could it be? Could it really be?
Was God sending the bird from above?
For it was like no bird I had ever seen,
Yet in a way it resembled a dove.

Slowly I walked the path to the house,
Trying to figure it all out in my mind;
Was God sending a message or warning me,
Or was my mind working overtime?

Again I spoke not a word of this
But when at last I was alone,
I fell on my knees and prayed, "O God!
If it is you, please make it known."

All the day long I searched the Scripture
And prayed, if it were His will,
God would fill my cup with answers I needed,
But no answers did He reveal.

Was I hearing things that were not there?
I knew of no one that had heard God speak.
Was the voice my imagination
Due to my soul's being weak?

After hours my weary body and mind
At last fell into slumber that night,
Then my blessed Lord appeared in a dream—
He came in splendor through a brilliant light.

"Yes, it was I that visited with you,
Both times it was I that came;
You heard my voice and you replied
Each time I spoke your name.

For weeks I have listened to your humble prayers,
You seek My help each time you pray;
I came this night to let you know
I am with you each hour of the day.

To prove the purity of my love
I sent the beautiful snow white dove;
All I ask of you is your faithfulness
And keep in your heart what I've revealed from above.

You turned not away when I beckoned to you,
You have searched your heart and soul;
But most of all, you have kept your faith
Though my coming was not foretold."

With this He ascended into the sky,
His raiments as white as the snow;
It seemed as He rose the clouds parted
As I stood there and watched Him go.

I awoke from the dream with a lightened heart
And with peace I had never known;
God had filled my cup full of understanding—
From this day forward, I'd never be alone.

Though I never again heard God's voice speak my name,
I've felt His presence from within;
I know without doubt when once more He calls,
Eternity for me will begin.

A MOTHER'S FAITH

Day after day she sat on her porch,
Waiting for the mailman to come,
Hoping and praying someone would write,
Someone that once knew her son.

Many years had passed since he went away
To fight in that awful war,
To do his part so that we could stay free
And keep bloodshed off our shore.

Once a week she received a letter from him
For about two years, I would say;
Oh, how happy she was when the letters came—
She read them over and over each day.

Then a week went by with no letter from him
And she thought, "He's too busy to write."
The weeks turned into months and still no word,
Yet she kept telling herself, "He's all right."

Then late one evening a telegram came,
The "We are sorry to inform you" kind;
With it clutched tightly in her hand
She just sat there a long, long time.

As she finally opened the telegram
These words the dear mother read:
"Missing in action"—her only child,
But she uttered, "Thank God, he's not dead."

As the years passed she patiently waited
For her dear son to come home;
And daily she prayed, "Watch over him, Lord."
Oh, the dear mother's faith was so strong!

She never lost hope that someday he'd return
For in her heart she knew he was alive,
And notification had never come
Telling her that her son had died.

Through the agony of not knowing the fate of her son
She had aged long before her time;
In the ten years of waiting her hair had turned white
And her face was now covered with lines.

Each morning she waited at her front door
For the mailman came by around nine;
Oh, how he wished he could bring her good news,
He'd watched her suffer for such a long time.

It was late summer and she was on her porch
With his picture clutched tight in her hand,
When off in the distance, walking up the road,
She could see the figure of a man.

Her old heart started pounding till she could hardly breathe
And she prayed, "Oh, God, is it true?"
As the man came nearer the dear mother shouted,
"Oh, Son! Oh, Son! Is it you?"

Indeed it was—her dear son was home,
The long years of waiting had passed;
He now walks with a cane and his hearing's almost gone,
But God spared him and he's home at last.

GOD LED ME

I must have made a wrong turn back there—
I've been driving for miles on this road;
I'm sure the arrow pointed this way,
But so far I haven't seen a soul.

I was getting worried and a little scared,
And thought, "I'll turn and go back,"
When out of nowhere, sitting back in the trees
Up ahead was a little old shack.

"Thank You, dear Lord," I uttered,
"You have never once let me down;
I don't know why I doubted now,
When I need You, You're always around."

As I walked the path to the little old shack,
I wondered why God led me here;
But it didn't take long to understand,
For very soon the answer was clear.

As I stood at the door and looked inside,
I thought, "Oh, God, why me?"
There on a cot was a small form,
And a little girl by the cot on her knee.

I walked over and saw a young lady,
About thirty, I would guess, on the cot;
As I put my arms around the little girl,
She said, "Mommy is all I've got.

Please help her, lady, please make her well,
My mommy is so sick today."
I knelt down beside the frail lady,
And this is what I heard her say.

"I know you have come to help us,
God assured me He'd send someone.
You see, there's no family to leave her with,
And I just couldn't leave her alone.

Please take my baby and care for her,
You see, she is not yet half-grown;
Oh, lady, she'll be no trouble to you—
God has beckoned and I must go home."

My heart was breaking in two now
And I prayed, "God, what must I do?"
When a voice seemed to come from nowhere,
Saying, "Fear not, I'll lead you."

I looked down at the frail form below me,
A smile was now on her face;
I knew God had taken her to heaven
To be in her rightful place.

It was late October when we laid her to rest,
The preacher, the little girl and I.
With tears in her eyes the little girl asked,
"Did God take mommy to the sky?"

I knelt down beside this precious child,
And held her as close as could be;
"Yes, God took her to heaven,
And He wants you to come home with me."

Many years have passed since I made that wrong turn
And God led me to that shack that day;
I know in my heart God led me there,
You see—the arrow points the other way.

THE OL' PHOTO ALBUM

An auction was held not far from my home,
It was to settle an estate.
I had nothing to do so I stopped by;
As I arrived I heard the auctioneer say,

"Who'll give me three for this ol' album?
Come on, folks, let's get underway;
Everything here must be sold at some price—
Who'll give me three for this album today?"

No bids were made so the auctioneer asked,
"Tell me, just what price will you pay?"
"I'll give you three." Then the auctioneer shouted,
"Sold to that lady in gray."

I do not know why I bid on the book,
I just felt it should not be sold;
Three dollars was the value of memories,
Stored for years by some dear ol' soul.

As the auctioneer placed the ol' album in my hands,
I had a feeling I'd never had before;
It was as if someone was saying,
"In this book my possessions I store."

Faded with years and worn from use,
The ol' album belonged to me;
Three dollars purchased the precious memories
Of someone I would never meet.

Upon arriving home I inspected my book—
I just couldn't believe my eyes;
It was handmade and covered in satin,
Now tattered and grayed by years gone by.

As I opened the album my eyes overflowed
As I sat there a while and cried;
Inside the cover, carved in the wood,
Were these words from a man to his bride.

"To My Beloved Wife, Gracie, on Our Wedding Day,
Who Shall Forever Be a Part of Me;
On the Fifth Day of June, Eighteen Eighty-Nine;
With Everlasting Love, Lee."

I shall never understand the reason
For allowing the ol' album sold;
No one wanted a tattered and faded ol' book,
What they wanted was silver and gold.

Only three dollars purchased this old book
That has meant so much to me;
No one will know the pleasure it has brought,
Except Gracie and possibly Lee.

THE LITTLE BOY ON THE STREET

"Why do you weep, my son?"
I asked a small boy on the street.
With tears streaming down his face he looked up
And reluctantly said to me,
"Who are you, Mister? Do I know you?"
I smiled and said, "Not as yet;
Tell me, son, what is your name?
I think it is time we met."

He just sat silent, so frail and small,
His clothes were ragged and torn;
The shoes on his feet were much too small
And both were badly worn;
"Do you live close by?" I asked him.
"It's getting quite late, you know;
Your daddy and mommy will worry about you—
Don't you think it's about time we go?"

I couldn't understand the look on his face
Nor the sadness that was in his eyes,
But as he spoke these words to me
I was beginning to realize.
"Mommy's gone to live in heaven,
I loved her so much, you know;
Tell me, Mister, why did she leave me?
Why, she knew I would want to go.

My daddy is home but he's drunk all the time
Since mommy left and went away.
Oh, I wish she'd come back and get me—
I wait on this corner each day;
Mommy used to talk to God all the time
And she said God loves me too;
I'll wait here so He can see me,
'Cause I don't know what else to do."

So frail he was just sitting there,
He looked so weak and small.
Oh, how my heart ached for this little child,
And no words would come to me at all;
So I sat beside him on the corner
And reached out and took his hand;
Together we'll wait for as long as it takes
For this child to understand.

THE WORLD THAT USED TO BE

Not long ago while touring the mountains
In the state of Tennessee,
I saw a sight I shall never forget—
It left such an impression on me.

At the foot of a mountain stood an old farmhouse,
Weather-worn and in need of repair,
And rocking very slowly on a big country porch
Was an old lady with snow white hair.

Her face was half covered with an old-fashioned bonnet
And her dress was down to the floor;
I felt as if I were viewing a painting
Of a world that existed no more.

Not a blade of grass could be seen in her yard,
Yet it was as neat as could be;
It looked as if it had just been swept
And it was shaded by a big oak tree.

The yard was enclosed by a split-rail fence
Separating it from a once-tended farm;
Way in the back of the old farmhouse,
Barely in view, was a half-standing barn.

Encircling the trunk of the large oak tree
Were flowers in bloom at the time;
In front of the porch was a row of lilies,
Neatly growing in a straight line.

I waved at the dear little lady,
She smiled and waved back at me;
And I thought, what peace and contentment
In the world that used to be.

I shall always remember that beautiful place
And the serenity that came over me,
When I viewed the world of that dear little lady,
The world that used to be.

GOD WALKED THE STAIRWAY OF HEAVEN

God walked the stairway of heaven
With a baby in His arms;
Looking down upon the sinful world,
He could see there was cause for alarm.

God had given so much to His children,
And it was hard to understand
Why wickedness was everywhere
Upon the face of the land.

Through the windows of heaven God watched.
"Why do they doubt My power and My way?
I love them so but they must understand
That my wishes they must obey."

Then He gazed at the precious baby.
"Do I dare to send My only Son
To rid the world of evil ways
And tell them of things to come?"

Fast asleep Jesus lay in His father's arms.
Oh, what a task He was soon to begin,
Faced with the salvation of all mankind,
And on His shoulders He would bear our sin.

Then God saw Mary and knew she was righteous;
He sent an angel this message to bring:
"Blessed art thou among women."
God chose Mary to bear Jesus our King.

A humble birth was that of our Savior,
In Bethlehem on a bright starry night;
In a stable Mary bore God's only Son,
While a star marked the place with its light.

Jesus grew in wisdom and stature,
And as He walked the roads of life
He told of God's love and deep concern
For man in this world filled with strife.

He told how His Heavenly Father
Had sent Him to save each of them;
He warned them to turn from their wicked ways
And to trust and follow Him.

Many miracles He performed along the way;
He was "The Man from Galilee."
By the gentle touch of His blessed hands
The lame could walk and the blind could see.

The highest price that could be paid,
Jesus paid, our souls to save;
He shed His life's blood for each of us;
He died, but He conquered the grave.

Now Jesus walks the stairway of heaven
Beside God on this very day;
Because of God's love He sent His Son
To save us, the sheep that went astray.

THE TATTERED OLD BOOK

In a very small room she sits alone,
Rocking slowing in an old rocking chair;
Her face and hands are wrinkled with time,
And the whitest of white is her hair.

Around her stooped shoulders she is wearing a shawl
Made of lace and very old;
In her frail hands is a tattered old book,
Worth much more to her than gold.

The tattered old book is a photo album,
Dating back over forty years;
So gently she turns one page at a time
And relives each with smiles and tears.

Inside the old book are her treasures,
Treasures that help her survive;
For with each photo there is a memory,
And her memories help keep her alive.

Through the pages of the tattered old book
She is young with many charms;
Her children once more are her children,
Still needing her loving arms.

Her years of raising a family are gone,
But in her daydreams they need her still;
She brings them back every now and then
Through memories that appear very real.

Stop and think—have you met this lady?
Does she sound familiar to you?
Could it possibly be your precious mother,
Who sits alone with nothing to do?

Is she doomed to live her remaining days
In the world that is now our past?
If the description fits your precious mother,
Just how long do you think she will last?

It costs so little to bring happiness to her;
Remember—her love is true.
All that it takes to warm her old heart
Is a simple "Mother, I love you."

A LITTLE GIRL'S PRAYER

Why these words have come to me,
This I do not know,
But in my heart I felt compelled
To listen to them flow.
A little girl so frail and small
With hair of golden strands
Sat in a tiny wheelchair;
A book lay in her hands.

The book lay there unopened
As she gazed across the way,
For through the window she could see
Little children run and play.
She never knew what it was like
To have her feet touch ground,
Or what it really felt like
To play and run around.

She did not know what it was like
To play a childhood game,
For most of her young life was spent
In agony and pain.
This was the only life she knew,
So little did she say,
But something seemed to bother her,
As she watched the children play.

In her six short years of life
She never once complained;
She had a smile for everyone
That spoke or called her name.
But her smile was gone now
And in earnest she did pray;
As she looked up to heaven
This is what I heard her say.

"Oh, Jesus, up in heaven,
I know I'm kinda small,
But mommy said You'd listen
To us, one and all.
You know I say my prayers
And I try hard to be good,
But something's wrong, dear Jesus,
Am I not doing what I should?

Why can't I be like others?
Why can't I run and play?
I get so tired of sitting
In my wheelchair every day.
Could we talk this over, Jesus?
I need You very bad.
Mommy's told me all about You;
If You'd come, I'd be so glad.

I know if You were here today,
You'd help someone like me,
'Cause mommy said that long ago
You made the blind man see.
But the thing that thrilled me most—
You made a lame man walk.
Oh, Jesus, that is why
I want to have this talk.

'Pick up your bed and walk'—
That's all he had to do
After You had blessed him,
So will You bless me too?
I don't think I'm strong enough
To pick up my bed and walk,
But I would try so very hard
If we could have our talk.

I thought that just maybe,
If You had the time to come,
I'd go back with you to heaven
Where I could have some fun.
I'd come by myself
But I'm 'fraid, since I'm so small,
And when I ask someone to take me,
They just smile and that is all.

One day I asked my mommy
To take me on a plane,
So I could fly to heaven
Where there'd be no more pain.
I'm sorry that I asked her,
'Cause it made her feel so bad,
She hugged me, then she cried all day
And ever since she looks so sad.

But if mommy could come with me,
She'd be happy as could be,
'Cause she's never seen me walk
And she'd be so proud of me.
I feel so very tired now,
I can't stay up very long,
But if I was there in heaven,
You'd make me well and strong.

I won't be a bit of trouble,
And I'll stay out of Your way.
Why, when my legs are well
I'll be walking all the day.
And I could help You, Jesus,
While You're hearing people pray.
I will sweep the streets of gold
In case someone comes to stay.

I'm so tired, dear Jesus,
I will sleep now for a while,
Just wake me up when You come—"
She uttered with a smile.
Well, no more will she suffer,
Jesus answered her sweet prayers.
She no longer needs a wheelchair
For she walks the golden stairs.

While the humble child lay sleeping,
Jesus beckoned her to come.
She will awake in heaven—
Her battle has been won.
All that knew this precious child,
Though saddened they will be,
Should rejoice in the knowledge
That Jesus set her free.